D0469822

We all need room to process our pain—a small space for big, hard things, and an addition out back for the joy and learning that often move in at the same time. Ashmae builds this for us with her words. We all need this book.

—Annie K Blake, artist
anniekblake.com

Hoiland reminds her readers to observe their ordinary lives with extraordinary attention. While this important work confronts the weight of a life-altering diagnosis, we are generously invited into Hoiland's unusually vibrant world, where her joy is as vivid as her pain.

—Kate Finlinson, writer

Hoiland connects with what's holy in a rare but enviable way. Rather than telling us what she knows, she tells us what she sees. And her eyes are wide open—to joy, to suffering, to the brevity of all things human, to the costs of being remade in the image of God.

—Adam S. Miller
author of *Letters to a Young Mormon*

A New Constellation

By Common Consent Press is a non-profit publisher dedicated to producing affordable, high-quality books that help define and shape the Latter-day Saint experience. BCC Press publishes books that address all aspects of Mormon life. Our mission includes finding manuscripts that will contribute to the lives of thoughtful Latter-day Saints, mentoring authors and nurturing projects to completion, and distributing important books to the Mormon audience at the lowest possible cost.

A New Constellation

A Memoir About a Beginning

Ashley Mae Hoiland

**BCC
PRESS**

A New Constellation: A Memoir About a Beginning
Copyright © 2019 by Ashley Mae Hoiland

All rights reserved. Printed in the United States of America. No part
of this book may be used or reproduced in any manner whatsoever
without written permission except in the case of brief quotations
embodied in critical articles or reviews.

For information contact
By Common Consent Press
4062 S. Evelyn Dr.
Salt Lake City, UT 84124-2250

Cover design: Clark Goldsberry with painting by Ashley Mae Hoiland
Book design: Andrew Heiss

www.bccpress.org

ISBN-10: 1-948218-14-3
ISBN-13: 978-1-948218-14-6

10 9 8 7 6 5 4 3 2 1

This book is for my Remy, Thea, Luna and Carl, who will take this journey with me whether they chose it or not.

For my parents, who I know would choose to every time.

And for the Jacaranda tree in my front yard who blooms purple flowers, expecting nothing in return.

Foreword

Reija Rawle, MD MS

The day I read this book I did several ordinary things. I woke up under a soft comforter in the dark to the sound of my baby son crying. I dressed all three of my children and fed them breakfast—Cheerios, milk, and veggie sticks. I went to work in a small medical clinic on the side of the highway with a meadow on one side and a mountain on the other. I met with a man who told me, as tears rolled down his cheeks, "There isn't a mountain in America I haven't been up and down, but now I can't walk even a few steps without pain." I met with a woman who had been attacked by an animal decades before and had her face rebuilt five times. "Girl," she said to me, "When you've had your own face change so many times you know how to read faces, you know." I ate yogurt with mini chocolate chips while I put down in the medical records her story, and his story, and all the other stories I collected that day in my work as a family physician. I like to think of my work this way: as a story-listener, a story-recorder, and sometimes a little story-writer.

When I left the clinic the sky was surprisingly light with a faint pink creeping up the hillsides. Climbing out of my minivan outside the daycare center I saw a flash of red wings—a cardinal. Years ago in medical school in upstate New York I learned that the first color of spring is not green, it is red. Red is last color to leave in the winter and the first to return. I felt a bit of hope stir in my heart—this frozen landscape will live again. I took my two youngest children to pick up my oldest. He goes to kindergarten in a set of low brown buildings on the edge of a forest where "the kinders" go hiking every Tuesday afternoon. We found him in the art building and ended up lingering after all the other children left as he mixed up colors into a thick bronzy gold and we poured it into a baby food jar so he could take it home to paint his cardboard "airplane" in our living room. Teacher Ben fed my baby pretzels as he swept the floor and for a few minutes I felt known, like the Earth had opened up that space, that time, that room just for me.

When we got home I left the baby with my husband and ran down the street with my oldest two to the fancy theater on the college campus where we live. My son's school was staging their musical production of "The Wizard of Oz." We got there just in time to find seats in front of my son's classmate, a redheaded freckled girl whose sixth birthday was one week before. I gave her a copy of the third Nancy Drew book from the used bookstore in our tiny downtown. During the play she leaned forward periodically and wrapped her arms around my neck while I put my hand across my chest and held her hand for a few seconds at a time. At one point the stage crew rolled out a green curtain on a clothes rack with a huge cardboard head of the student playing Oz and it was, for unclear reasons, universally hilarious. Everyone in the audience started to laugh. While I was laughing I turned around and saw a few rows back and to my left one of my patients, a tall thin lady who has multiple sclerosis. "Are you seeing a neurologist for treatments?" I had asked when I met her. "No," she replied, "I just try to get up everyday and move as much as I can." So there she was, sitting and laughing and rocking back and forth in her seat just like the rest of us. You never would have known.

After the play I raced my children home in the cold twilight. When we moved to our small college town from the big city I wanted the sky to be an explosion of stars, but there are too many beautiful clouds. I try not to mind but still I want to push them away—I want to see farther than I can see now. Before bed, I read my son the first chapters of "Redwall" and grew very hungry in just the first few pages. I ate a piece of chocolate, did the dishes, brushed my teeth and got into bed but got distracted and made love with my husband under the soft comforter. When we were done he went up to the attic to work for a while. I looked at my phone to set the alarm and found this book waiting in my email so I read it right then and there, on the small screen of my phone, in the dark, wrapped up and warm in my bed. When I finished I wanted to cheer loudly but instead I fell peacefully asleep, full of love for this beautiful little book and its author, who left soup and bread tied to my bicycle handlebars on the first night we met almost a decade ago.

When you finish this book, you will also want to cheer or perhaps you'll want to cry. Perhaps you'll want to sleep. Whatever you do, please take a pencil and begin to write. Write in the margins of the book or in your own journal. Smudge the pages with graphite and bits of eraser but don't stop until you've put down your story, whatever story you want to tell. The story of the day you read the book, the day you were born into sorrow, or the day you carried another person alight on your gentle wings. Let your words flow into the river of kindness that runs from these pages, then let them settle down in the eddies of your heart where you can find them again in your time of need. Before closing the book, turn the final page with your thumb and run your fingers over the spine as if it were your own. You'll know yourself better for having made your own record. For you have a story and it is yours to tell.

The World Changes Without Warning

When my daughter finally crossed the monkey bars on her
   own,
I thought the world would surely want to know
the way she created her own momentum,
the way her small hands gripped the blue metal bar
and when she was about to fall,
the way she adjusted her weight hanging in the air like that,
her whole body intent on finishing.
The way for a moment I saw her hang with one hand
and her strength surprised us both
but neither said a word.
The way she set her feet back on the earth at the end
and looked at me and both of us knew
she was not the same as she was one minute before.

This is everything and nothing. And everything and nothing. In a year, or in ten years, I may look back and see that my life did not change at all. Or it may be that everything shifts, and my body, my life, will look drastically different than the way it looks now. The heart does not know what it can hold until it is given the thing it must carry. I did not know I would love my children, or the ocean, or the purple flowers that bloom in our front yard tree, until they showed up for me, until I was asked to stoop down and take a piece of them into my heart. I imagine it is the same with things that are hard; I cannot dictate beforehand the ways they will contract and expand my universe until they show up at my front door unexpected. And then I will know they have traveled a long way to get here, that they have made plans to be here for this part of the journey, and that I must let them in.

So, if this is everything, okay. If it is nothing, okay. The closer I get to looking at the differences, the two ideas seem to be exactly the same.

I am looking at raw heartache in real time, however momentary. It feels important to give sadness credence and a space to be preserved. Like a slant of light that passed by so quickly, I had to reach out and hold on, to write it down so I knew it really existed. So many people have and will suffer a great deal more than me. So many are better acquainted with the ache of the heart, the brokenness of pieces, the loss of what once was. In every hurt there must exist some balm. Writing is mine.

It is a strange, but fairly inconsequential thing to have double vision out of one eye, or so I thought. It was a nuisance that made chasing my toddler through the fabric store days earlier a dizzying experience, but a nuisance at worst. While parking outside the optometrist's office for my first appointment, I heard a honk. Out the side of my eye I could see three of the same car, but I couldn't tell which one I was about to merge into. The driver of the other car corrected the mistake, not me, and I pulled into a spot hoping they would pass me without stopping.

I remembered feeling so clumsy just days before, at a class at the gym, like I couldn't get my body to do what I wanted it to. I remember feeling ashamed that I wasn't stronger, more coordinated, and I had promised myself I wouldn't go back to the class until I'd lost some weight.

And a couple of weeks earlier, while turning around to speak to my children in the car the night we got pizza and ate on the cliffs by the beach, I recognized that my clarity of thought, along with my vision, was jumbled, that the world was not as clear as it had always been for me. This change was jarring, but a mother does not have time for the jarring; she must glide smoothly through the world, her children following behind her. On a conscious level I didn't think twice about these mishaps. I wrote them off as stress, tiredness, getting older—but somewhere in the back of my head I had known for weeks that something was not right.

In the optometrist's office, I sat in the patient room as a nurse filled my eyes with a golden numbing liquid and dilated the pupils. I had no idea that a dilation means an actual stretch of the pupil. I felt like a chamber had been opened, the roundness tugged apart by the drops, pushing color to the edges. "Things will get blurry up close," she said. "Just sit in the waiting room for about twenty minutes, and the doctor will come get you."

I sat in my striped skirt, a grey sweatshirt with flowers, and the tall snow boots I found at Goodwill. Next to me was a tiny Christmas tree on a table, the lights blinking in and out of focus. I tried to look for Christmas gifts to purchase on Amazon, and could not see a thing. I've always had perfect vision, and suddenly I knew why my husband reaches so fervently for his glasses each morning. Around me in that tiny room were strangers. A man with dreadlocks typical of Santa Cruz surfers. A woman with her aged mother. An older man with rough, windburned cheeks. I was the youngest in the room. Our names were being called by nurses, all of us there for our eyes. So simple. I blinked a few times, feeling both alone and a part of something. The Christmas lights on the tree were blinking on and off, the little train around the base moving slowly. For the first time in my life, I was seeing everything as if I were looking through a thick glass. I settled into myself for that brief moment when it seemed futile to try and see things just as I always have.

I was called back into another room. The optometrist, Dr. Chaves, had a framed picture sitting on the desk of her, her husband, and a son the same age as my youngest. I liked her even before she came in. She had been a doctor for four years, and her degree was from Berkeley. I wondered if we were both new in this town. She was small and precise. I'd never had an eye exam, and as she stood in front of me I felt a moment of immense awe for what had taken place years, even decades before I got here in order for this kind doctor to look at my eyes—I mean actually to the back, the insides of my eyes. I wonder if she knew right away. She saw that my eye muscle was palsied, that I was not just mistaken or making things up (which I was sure the doctor would tell me) that the eye muscle just was not moving far enough to the side for me to see properly.

When I think about her now, I wonder what it is like to be the first on the front lines of bad news. I wonder if the people who perform this brave work are compensated in other ways. Maybe their beds are extra comfortable, or waiters more attentive, or they always find an available parking space right at the front. There must be some sort of universal kindness extended toward them because, while my doctor stayed totally calm, I now realize that she must have known right away that the work she did that morning—a moment of culmination for what she had long studied, prepared, worked for—would end with her telling me news I wasn't prepared to hear.

She called me later that day to see how things had gone with the MRI, and her voice was noticeably different when I shakily gave my answer. I don't think she was feigning sadness when she said how sorry she was. It is strange to me how indebted I still feel to the people who first shared this news with me:, the strangers who seemed to care more than their jobs required. The nurse in the ER who came in just once while Carl filled out some paperwork and, as she was leaving asked, "So what are you here for?" Carl told her about the diagnosis we'd received just an hour before, and the woman looked up with real tears in her eyes and said, "I'm so sorry, I didn't realize that was the news you received." Real tears, for me, a pathetic, puffy-eyed stranger on a thin bed in a tiny room at the place that pays her to come and work.

Again, there is an attentiveness that comes when the world shifts this way, when the news I was given felt like everything and nothing. Everything because I cannot go backwards to what it all was before this day, and nothing because I am still me, just as I have always been.

For maybe the only, and surely the first time I can remember, it seemed for those few hours that every power in the universe was focused in on me. It is both startling and changing. It makes me want to be present and ready just in case someone else needs me to enter their story and acknowledge their pain at just the right moment.

The drive home from that appointment should have given me nothing to worry about. Dr. Chavez had tucked her short, dark hair behind her ears and then put her hand in her lab coat as she told me just to keep my phone nearby, just in case. My eyes, blinking from the sunlight, which was so much more than I normally take in because of the dilation, were filled with tears though. Somewhere in a fold of my brain, tucked away like a letter I'd forgot to open, I knew that something was wrong.

We had moved to Santa Cruz three months earlier, and the landscape did not quite feel like my own yet. The beach had taken me in like an adopted sister, but I still felt weary of my dedication to stay near it. The palm trees and giant succulents felt like friends. The rescue dog owners at the dog park had been kind, and I'd even exchanged numbers with a few thinking our families might picnic together. I took pride in how easily I navigated this new city as I drove along the busy road toward home. The first months in a new place are vibrant and lonely. I've moved to enough new places to know that the first months unveil details that you cannot see later. Santa Cruz was no different.

The ocean, a staple and constant in our life, felt like a heartbeat that was used to change. It was both a comfort and a surprise that the same beach looked different every time we came back—a new stream running through the middle, attaching itself to the nervous system of ocean water through a thousand tiny veins. A cliff formed, and my children jumped from it endlessly, but when we came back it was flat sand. We went one stormy day, and the foam that came in with the tide covered their heads completely.

But these are the ways of oceans. The waves that crash up and over a rocky cliff on one afternoon are calm and lap the sides on the next. The tidepools we could walk along, bending to touch a starfish, are water-filled holes like windows into the earth, but on another morning those same cliffs are submerged by the high tide.

The beach and the mountains filled me up a pixel at a time, the everydayness of moving through a new place, walking up the street to the blue elementary school, the gym around the corner, the gulch with the muddy trails and three black cows grazing in the middle, the taco stand with bright pink shrimp, to the cliffs along the beach, all filling me up without my knowing.

I pulled into our cul-de-sac, hid my eyes behind sunglasses, and walked inside—but the yellow iodine from the numbing eye drops had stained my cheeks, like drops of sunlight my eyeballs could not hold. Life is like that. We are filled and filled, and at some point . . . it's not that it's too much, it's just apparent that we are full. Walking in the house after my appointment that day, I carried something that perhaps had always been written for me. Or was it a piece of story, needing a home, searching for someone to tell it when it found me?

I didn't know what else to do until the doctor called, so I pulled out the soft, pink dragon I had been sewing for my five-year old daughter, Thea, for Christmas. I began stitching the ears. With her whole heart, Thea wanted a real dragon that would hatch from a golden egg and do things like fly around the room and get her drinks of water. Despite my efforts to persuade her that a dragon needs to stay on the remote island where dragons avoid extinction, she put all her faith in both Santa Claus and

Jesus and rested comfortably with the notion that, since they both were capable of anything her heart could want, at least one of them would pull through.

I spent time puzzling out how to best help her navigate disappointment, which, as it turns out, is a main tenet of what I've learned to do as a parent. In my puzzling, I finally realized something important—the point for Thea was not her desire for a real dragon that would sleep on the bottom bunk and go on walks with our dog; the point was that Thea wanted someone to give credence to her words and ideas, however absurd they might have been. She wanted to know that someone heard her calling out from her place in the middle of our three children. I sensed that she wanted to feel special, wanted to know that some part of the universe set aside time just for her. So, while I awaited the doctor's return call, I stitched and sewed the ears and the horns with bright purple and pink fabric, and even if everything was about to change, I knew I was doing the only thing I should be doing at that moment.

My phone buzzed, and I tried to sound completely collected as Dr. Chavez told me to go to the emergency room, which, she said, was more dramatic sounding than it actually was. She would set up the MRI for me, and a neurologist would be there to read the reports. I had never been to the emergency room, and never imagined that, should such a day ever come, I would drive over calmly handing Ritz crackers to my baby in the backseat while discussing some political topic with Carl. I didn't imagine that I would walk into an empty waiting room. And I could never have dreamed up the woman with the maroon dyed hair pulled back into a ponytail without affair, who waited behind the counter to take my information wearing the same bright orange scrub top that everybody else in the office wore. How we ended up skimming across each another's universes seems a miracle to me. I've encountered this miracle again and again in my life, but in these first weeks, I feel I am a little more tuned in to the hum of suffering that is carried on the air of every place. This, in turn, means that I am also a little likely to see "miracle" as the proper word for someone who is kinder than I expect them to be.

She called me lovey and sweetheart, words which might have felt pejorative or too small in another time and place but were right for that moment. I wanted to believe that she really felt that I was worthy of those words. I wanted to believe she saw something golden inside of me. I was also struck with the thought of how few times I had called someone else lovey or sweetheart in the past. I had used all sorts of fancy names for people and things, mostly having to do with what they had accomplished, or graduated from, or created, but lovey and sweetheart had not made the top of any of my lists because anyone can get those names just by being alive.

And so it is with suffering, as you enter in under that wing and allow the warmth of weight to pull you in tight. You allow yourself titles like lovey and sweetheart because, what else would you want to be called in such a moment? All the other titles suddenly and momentarily seemed a waste of time.

Why would I need another title, another accolade, in my most humble moment. A woman in an orange scrub top and a short ponytail is looking at me as if I were the most lovable creature alive and telling me how beautiful my baby is, and calling me the names I thought I'd grown out of, but needed all along. What could be more important than this?

In the eight hours following my arrival at the ER, many things happened. But also, hardly anything happened. A woman took my blood pressure; it was normal. Another woman, an intern, seemed giddy to hear about my dilated eye and the muscle that was palsied. She asked to look inside because it's not every day you get to see such wonders. I let her. I felt generous and brave sitting in the padded chair while she shone the light into my pupil. I went and sat on a bed in a small room. A woman with an ice pack covering her ankle rolled by in a wheelchair, and I thought, "Thank goodness that isn't me." Another nurse came in and touched the veins on the inside of my arm. She was as gentle as the brush of a wing against my cold skin and retreating veins. Even with her kindness, I was light-headed, pale, and crying. Needles were used. Blood was drawn. An IV was placed. An MRI was completed on the second try, after more anti-anxiety medication was given.

I lay with my eyes closed, without moving, in the MRI machine. It was so loud, a real racket, but I swear, somewhere behind it all I heard the tune of a grand piano. And hovering outside the machine, one near my feet and one near the light by my head, I pictured my two grandmothers floating in the air, coming under the closed door, not speaking, but reaching down intermittently. I did not open my eyes while the giant magnets of the MRI swooshed around me. I learned later that all the noise comes from the magnetic force switching directions over and over. Because the change in magnetic force is so rapid and intense, some people experience sensations that feel like someone reaching out and touching them. Of course, no one is there, but in this other worldly metallic womb, in this other worldly moment, I did not feel alone.

I kept my eyes closed until I was wheeled out across the parking lot and I felt the sun on my eyelids. I remember looking up to see a handsome Latino boy, early twenties, pushing my hospital gurney. I immediately felt self-conscious and dumb, there in that hospital gown, with no bra and only a thin sheet covering me. A clear sense of fear lurked behind the calm I was trying to emit.

The boy smiled down at me once and then looked ahead. He navigated around perfectly hedged bushes, gently up and over a curb, through the many sidewalks, and back to my room holding his security card against the doors until they opened. Again, I felt so silly. I wanted to tell him that I could just walk, that he didn't need to go to all this trouble, but my head was pounding, and the glow-in-the-dark dye they'd put in my veins for the MRI was still swirling through my body. So here I was, on a bed with wheels, being pushed by a clean-cut boy at least ten years younger than me. The wide openness of vulnerability lay on me as still as the sheet pulled up to my chin. But before he made the final turn back into my room, I remember looking at the boy doing his job and thinking, "Wow, this is what we do for each other."

I waited alone in the small room again. Full of headache and nausea. I wished I'd eaten breakfast those many hours earlier when I thought the day was just another day. The nurse, maroon hair, bright orange scrubs, came into my room with a paper and a number circled in highlighter. "I hate to ask this," she said. "It's the worst part of my job, but can you pay this amount now?" I could not. Just weeks before Carl had defended his dissertation, and we were without steady income for the time being. Christmas was six days away, and finances were tight. It was likely a concoction of medication, double vision, and a general feeling of being overwhelmed, but I did not answer her in words. I just started to cry.

Only part of me was crying about the money; a larger part of me was crying because this woman was so tender, moving around me like a cat watching over her kitten. Once again, she did not need to be so kind, and once again she was. She patted my arm and said, "I'm just going to go put this in the shredder. Now is not the time." Minutes later she returned with a soft, stuffed giraffe and tucked it under my arm. "To keep you company," she said. Again and again, this is what we do for each other. The world broke open to me and all the people held me up like a blue porcelain platter my mother used to fill with warm chocolate chip cookies when I came home with my friends after school.

I guess I thought there would be a little more fanfare, a little more of a pause in the world—maybe a team of people crowding into the room and the other ER patients listening for my results—when the nurse finally came back from radiology with a paper in her hand. None of that happened, though. Carl had just come back in the room after dropping Hilde, our youngest, off at a babysitter's. I was in the bed, red-eyed, a stuffed giraffe under my arm. I assumed, as most things in my life have gone, that it would all be nothing. This day would be for naught, and my double vision and the numbness in my left side would just go away.

I was not prepared for the nurse with the paper in her hand—one I had not yet seen and would never see again. She entered the room without even closing the door, shuffled some supplies around the tiny sink and counter, sat in a chair, and said a simple sentence that was no more than a few words strung together in the air between us. While looking right at me, she said, "We will run one more blood test, but all signs are indicative of MS."

I keep going back in my memory trying to remember her reaction, her face, her voice, but I cannot remember any of it. She didn't stay in the room, but I don't know when she left. She did close the door on her way out though. It was just me and Carl and that new sentence still hanging in the air, filling in the space where the nurse had been. I remember my face contorting in a way it hasn't before, and I cried loudly, which I never do. It felt so ugly, so out of character, that I feel a little embarrassed when I think of it now.

Then I didn't know what to do. Carl, who always knows what to do, was calm, and I don't doubt that my hand was in his. I'm sure from experience, though I can't remember the details, that Carl sat on the edge of the bed next to me and said something useful. If there is a way to prepare yourself for the shock of news that is unexpected and life altering, I do not know what this preparation looks like. I had never considered what my steps immediately following such news would be, and so it was all an act of improvisation right there in that hospital room.

My world cracked, and all I could think of was a friend from high school—the one with the angelic singing voice, the one who sang "God is Love" at a morning devotional. I thought of her and how, when she posted to social media that she had been diagnosed with MS a year before, I didn't even respond with a comment because I didn't know what to say, because I was so glad it wasn't me.

Diagnosis

How long have I been sheathing and un-sheathing things
that matter to me?

A close-fitting cover to protect something—
The rainbow blanket I place around and under my sleeping
baby each night.
God.
Sadness a blade inside a cover, for all of us, I think.
We un-sheath it and cut through the overgrowth to get the
meadow on the other side.

And today I learned that even inside my brain,
A micro un-sheathing has been happening without my
knowing.
Taking muscles from my right eye, my left hand, the cold
spot on my cheek.
I do not know how to command them to cover up again,
those nerves.
The nerve.

I trust the work the body does, the hot tectonic shifting I can
barely detect,
Breaking apart the only Pangea I ever knew
And trust it will re-arrange itself into something of a new
history,
One that is mine to write.

I **want to tell everyone** I see so they can quickly build a net to catch me in, and I never want to talk about this diagnosis ever again. I imagine that this dance must happen with all hard things, moving in and out of what once was and what now is. I steep myself in memories that felt safer, but the flavor in the cup is changing, becoming more robust; the past, present and future are combining into a warmness that I never imagined would be the thing that I hoped would make me wise.

I **am also ashamed** at the many ways that I did not listen to the hum of suffering that my own charmed and privileged life allowed me to not need to hear for so long. I am sorry. I was mistaken to believe that none of it had to do with me.

After almost twelve hours at the ER, Carl and I got in the car and drove home from the hospital. My arm was still sticky with tape, bruises were already starting to show in the hollow of my elbow, my eyes were swollen and red, and I knew that I didn't want to fall apart in front of my children. I braced myself against the seat and breathed slowly, as I do before reading to a crowd. I could see lights on in the kitchen as we pulled into the driveway. Joel, our housemate, and Carl's business partner, and his girlfriend Deborah had spent the day with all three of the kids. Nets are woven so quickly. I did not cry when I walked in the door, perhaps because the immediate chaos and mess of small children rushed at me, and I re-materialized into only a mother again. Something, a bit of adrenaline perhaps, held me together.

It was a day after Deborah's birthday, and the kids had frosted a cake for her with the frosting I'd made and put in a bowl the night before. Thea poured sprinkles into her hand and laid them carefully in red, green and white strips across the frosting. That image—her so deliberately pouring shimmers from her five-year old palm—pulled me back to the earth and even beyond. It pulled me, for the dozenth time that day, through the small crack that had opened in the earth. I floated there in the kitchen watching the life that was mine, the people who were mine. Everything was exactly the same, and somehow everything was different.

After we sang and ate cake, I tucked the kids into bed, and the act felt far more important than it actually was. I was determined to keep moving, to thrust myself into the momentum of the quotidiana I know so well, and I stepped out into the hallway to put something in the laundry. Joel was sweeping the kitchen floor as I passed. "I'm so sorry," he said, and reached out to give me a hug. I stepped into it without question. It was long and without words, and I cried in my house for the second time that day. I realized that I had never hugged him before and that weight of another person against my own new body again ushered me to that space under the wing. For so long I had been invincible. I was the caretaker, the one in charge, the oldest of four, the captain of the soccer team, the prom queen, the winner of the awards, the mom. I rode easily on the crest of the wing, looking out over the landscape, eager to fix things, to make people happy, to make a difference.

In that moment in the hallway, though, I retreated from all those things, or they backed away from me. There was a space I had not noticed before because I'd never had to access it. I climbed down off the wing and searched around for warmth. I found a good portion of the world I know huddled close down below, beneath that great wing. Both shadows and light. I was surprised to see who was there, especially those I had never heard speak of hardship. I was not surprised to see some other people there because their hardships were well-known, I just hadn't known this place existed.

This is something I learned almost directly after I slid down from on top of the wing in the hospital room: the space underneath was populated with wise people. They accepted me and my reason for showing up so suddenly without question or judgment, even if my circumstance was much less severe than theirs. I hadn't anticipated that people would show up in my real life, one by one, to offer simple apologies and hugs that felt like gifts. I couldn't have predicted my body leaning into each of them like I truly believed they might heal me.

I did not sleep the night I came home from the hospital. When I asked the nurse at the ER about the side effects of the steroid treatment I received, he said that there were none, and I believed him. But at 1 a.m. I was wide awake with sleep nowhere on the horizon.

I moved through the house quietly, Carl and the kids breathing into the still air, the heater in the hallway clicking off and on, the moon outside waxing to almost full. I wrote, the words rushing out of my temporarily breaking heart. Thea's pink dragon was waiting for me, incomplete, so I began to work. When the garage—where I took my sewing machine so no one would wake up—got too cold, I came inside and spent a long time with my computer open on my lap. I wrote poems and pages of words that surprised me. It was that first night that I huddled under the wing of the bird, just me and my ability to create, that I felt I would be okay.

At five a.m. I slid myself, cold feet and all, back into bed next to Carl. He felt the covers shift and woke up. In the morning light, I could see the edges of his movements, as gentle as a rabbit. He had not cried yet, and I wondered if and when he would. Where do people who are not at the center of the circle, but still so close to it, place their grief? Do they hand it off to someone in a place further beyond the epicenter without letting anyone else see? When do they cry? And where? To whom do they turn?

I still haven't seen him cry, but I wonder if his heart dropped at the same time as mine when we saw the man with MS at my parent's church stumble and clutch his walker as he made his way up the aisle toward us. If his heart dropped, he said nothing then or later. Hard things do not just happen to one person; they spread across the landscape of entire families like a blanket of December snow we watch from the windows of my parent's living room.

I **didn't sleep for days** after several more rounds of steroids. One night, I sat on the couch in the dark while everyone slept and opened up the Hubble Telescope advent calendar on my computer. Three images short of a complete set for Christmas. The images, rectangles of color on my screen, seemed imperative to study in that moment. They were a reminder that everything not known will someday be known. I wanted to keep these images, so I spent an hour in photoshop converting the files and sending the whole lot of them to Costco to be printed. I ordered copies for my sister and her family too, as if everyone would surely recognize how important they were.

I cannot explain why this act of looking at what I don't understand, but still find beautiful, felt like mercy. Perhaps I sensed a tangible thread of hope that there must be more, some endless universe who cares about magnificent color, about rings of light that pulse outward, or celestial bodies that smash together with such force that they form something entirely new. And surely some force, some energy who understood my arrival at this new beginning, was swirling in the darkness of a living room. I read this caption underneath Day 4 of the advent calendar, an image of a bright star in the darkness:

> A young star, IRAS 14568-6304, at center, is cloaked in a haze of golden gas and dust. It appears to be embedded in a swath of dark sky. This dark region is known as the Circinus molecular cloud, an object with a mass around 250,000 times that of the Sun, filled with gas, dust and young stars. The star IRAS 14568-6304 is driving a protostellar jet, which appears here as the "tail" below, made up of the leftover gas and dust that the star took from its parent cloud in order to form.

And somehow, in the newness of that night, in the shock of such a sharp pivot, these words seemed to be talking about and to me. Like scripture, like tarot, like prayers my ancient grandmothers say over me.

At some point in all this newness, I thought back to myself as a 21-year old Christian missionary in Uruguay. I remember so distinctly one house we used to visit. We wove through a series of shanty allies, corrugated tin roofs, skinny dogs, front doors that only half closed. Their house was hardly a house but more like a shed in a row of other half-crumbling cement sheds. I spent time with this family in the winter of 2006. Their mud floor was wet, cold, and hard as cement. The dark color of the mud and wooden walls cast shadows through the dingy dwelling. It is all a bit vague now, but I vividly recall the smell of dampness and stale bread, the bars on the windows, the three kids and parents who somehow etched out an existence in this slice of poverty in a town near the Brazilian border that no one will ever know or think about outside of that province.

This image comes back to me often because, somewhere inside of me, it still matters that this family carried that piece of earth—or that it carried them. They knew the intricacies of what belonged to them. I think of how they knew what was just beyond their neighborhood, the tiny grocery store on the corner that sold rolls of cookies; the butcher shop across the street that was painted white and smelled of blood; the church, fenced off and made of red brick. At the time I remember feeling sorry for this family. I remember thinking how little of this world they knew and owned and how sad that was to me. I could not, at the time, consider though how much it would mean to me years later to know a small plot of earth in a different hemisphere so intimately that I felt ownership over it. In the years after my mission, and particularly in the weeks after my diagnosis, the fact that I know the olive tree in my front yard well enough to go out and finger the leaves and let my heart flutter a little at the sight of a budding olive makes this trip to earth feel expansive and still only mine.

Some other things that I know are uniquely mine. Only I know about the Friday afternoon that my children and I went to Home Depot to pick out long planks of wood— that the man who was a stranger saw us heading to our car, took my cart, and loaded all of the wood for me into the trunk. Only I know how we gathered in the front yard and hammered and screwed, sanded and stained, until we had a sandbox. Only I own the muscle memory of carrying fifteen bags of play sand and dumping them into the box we built. That 6′×3′ plot of land is entirely inconsequential, like the home of the family from my mission, but my kids and I know it so well, and in the knowing we also love it.

Beyond the sandbox, the jacaranda tree above us, the hollyhocks that Thea and I planted in rows of seeds that now stand above her head, the hydrangeas that bloom in spring like balls of cotton candy, the cilantro in the garden, the tomato plant that produced one tomato before it withered, the flat, rock path to the road. All of this, even if temporary, is mine to care for and tell. And in light of my world shifting, that idea seems wholly a gift. I wish I could have realized this about the family I felt sorry for as a missionary. I wish I could have understood that they owned a piece of the earth, however small, that I did not and never could. I wish I'd better given credence to the gifts in front of me, even when they didn't match up with what I thought they should be in order to cherish. Here under the wing, however momentarily, I see this. I see that it is not my place to say what another person's experience means or does not mean. I only can see that they quietly tilled their plot of earth, likely doing the best they could, loving things I cannot see.

I wanted to go home to the place where I grew up. I wanted to move back to what I knew so well as a child. For nearly a decade we had been away in California, and not just in California, but in the heart of Silicon Valley at Stanford University. The environment and energy felt important and big. I felt invincible. I felt like I understood complexities and my brain was firing rapidly all the time. I loved it there. I could not picture myself back in Utah, back on the suburban street with the matching houses and the view of the muddy lake across the valley. My hometown felt like an insignificant and sometimes backward place that was still ensconced in a religion that felt increasingly distant from me. It did not carry the same excitement as Palo Alto. My hometown was not built on belief of the impossible like Palo Alto, or populated by freedom and choice like Santa Cruz. It was built on tradition and sustained by obedience, and I had been working hard to buck both.

We drove back to Utah for Christmas, toward that house in the suburbs I suddenly longed for, on the morning I finished my last steroid treatment. I had an absurd amount of adrenaline and energy from the medication, so I drove us straight through the Sierra mountains and on into the desert as night began to fall. The kids slept in little piles in the back seat, the black, cold sky without clouds tucked in around us. Again, our story, just ours, moving at eighty miles per hour through the quiet basins of northern Nevada.

Had it been light enough, Carl, who is a geologist, would have pointed out to me the road that winds up into the Ruby mountains. He always tells me how it doesn't look like much from the freeway, but once you are up there you can see secret lakes, green forests, 360 degree views from the top where you can see both basin and then range and then basin and so on and on to the Sierras or to the Wasatch. And then you can see both ancient and modern fault lines, and beneath your feet, the nearly unrecognizably deformed and metamorphosed rock layers that turn in on themselves like folds of the brain.

Carl's pace would pick up as he retold it, the wholesale rifting of the North American crust, the once-continuous stratigraphy full of fossils and untold stories now broken apart by the slowest of divergent motions, appearing to culminate at this very location where its deepest parts are now exposed. He always says that being a geologist is like reading the language of the earth. The mountain belts are the chapters, the evidence of tectonic shifts and ancient processes the paragraphs, the rocks themselves are the sentences, the minerals – like the tiny zircon he's spent years studying in his lab – are the words, and the atoms that make up everything are the letters. I pause.... My neurons, then, are the words. And my mountains will erode like all others.

Just weeks before this drive through the desert, the day I noticed that my eye had double vision, Carl had defended his dissertation to a roomful of scientists and friends in the geology library in a corner of campus. Watching him from the audience, I again sensed that he had access to so many stories I did not know. He loves the millions of years it takes to form something new. He loves the garnets he spent summers searching for to bring back and analyze. The garnets, in particular, are like little time capsules, retaining information about what pressures and temperatures the rocks in which they were found were formed at.

To anyone else, these garnets would seem like just another mineral. To Carl, they are ancient, miniature Bibles that he spent seven years peering into, learning the language, trying to decipher what it all means. I admire his dedication to telling the story of the mountains four hours west of my hometown—and so far beyond any landscape I ever considered, a landscape most people will never think or care about at all.

As he gave his hour-long talk in front of that audience. I recognized that what he does sits on the point of a pin, but at the same time, the questions he is asking of his single set of rocks in the Nevada desert has significance far beyond its location. What he says will either build upon or tear down a piece of what scientists have thought they have known for decades. Carl is pushing against the earth's story and then putting his ear to the ground to see what is told back. Some of the answers that came after his years of digging for them were surprising to every scientist in that room. Sometimes even he is hesitant to believe his own data, which suggests the garnets, which were thought to have been created by the high pressures experienced when buried tens of miles below the earth's surface, were in fact never buried far down at all. Instead, it seems they had always stayed relatively close to the surface and had been squeezed with incredible pressure from the sides until they resembled something that was previously thought to have been only possible below the weight of a mountain range resembling the Himalayas.

I guess the point, then, is that the thing that I think I know is likely not the thing that I actually do. The point is that I cannot know the story I am about to live. I can only prepare myself to witness it, examine it, and be willing to be surprised by it. And however local and insignificant my ground may seem, it is relevant because all stories are relevant. Every story matters.

Carl tended to a forgotten piece of land until it told him something that he did not know before. He patiently ran the failed experiments and went back each summer to hike through the heat alone to gather more samples. He lived in his advisor's office for three weeks that last summer while the kids and I were in Utah and our housing had run out. He ran one final, desperate experiment to clarify what he had spent seven years trying to understand, and it worked. The complicated machines that filled two entire rooms and involved lasers, small vacuum chambers, and powerful magnets ultimately had the ability to say just how many millions of years before, and under how much pressure, a garnet had been formed.

The answers came, but not in they way he had planned—and not in the way that he had wanted so many years earlier. I know he gets embarrassed at times about the insignificance of the work that he does as theoretical geologist. And sometimes I am not patient about his work either. That morning, sitting on the padded chair out in the audience while he presented the work of his dissertation, I did not know that I was also on the precipice of change—even if the whole story had already been written in my DNA. I did not know that the pressures that would form my story into something as surprising as a garnet in the desert would not come from the places I assumed they would. I did not know that everything would be more complicated, more complex, and more difficult to understand than a chronological story about what it is to be a human in this world.

I've come to understand that Carl's geological work sometimes feels unimportant to me because I can't understand how can a single spot out in the mountains of a desert can matter so much. Why spend the time there? But I've often heard him use the phrase, "type locality," which refers to the first place where a particular phenomenon is discovered, often reaching outward to shed light on similar processes and areas in different parts of the world. I am not the type locality for sickness or hardship, or even for someone who has faced something unexpected. But

I am my own type locality. I am unearthing newness for myself in this space. The nexus of webbing this creates is complex. We are excavating newness, a different way of reading both our history and our future, and shaping our story over and over into what we didn't know it could be.

When we finally pulled into my parent's driveway at three a.m., after the straight-through drive from California, the air was bitter cold, and I was finally tired. We immediately went to the work of gathering up the sleeping hills of our three children and tucking them into the bed my mom had made for them. Remy and Thea both woke up long enough to recognize that they were in their grandparents house, little Christmas lights taped above them on the wall. My mom, grandma, had made up their bed with the softest blankets and put the two stuffed plush pug dogs on their pillows.

Of course, both my parents had waited up for us even though we told them to go to bed, and my Dad, grandpa, even with his limp knee from the motorcycle accident the previous year, insisted on unloading and carrying in the heaviest suitcase.

After the hustle of arrival settled I walked out of my parent's front door to grab one last thing from the car, and I looked up at the mountain ridge behind the house I grew up in. We lived right on the alluvial fan at the base of this particular and non-descript mountain. I don't even know its name, even though I spent much of my youth and early adulthood scrambling up the rocks and paths of its wide body. I had a moment of gathering in that settled me. I knew the rocks that jutted up in a diagonal to the top, the one spindly tree that still stood silhouetted against the sky on the upper ridge. The place, long grown over, where a lone pilot had flown himself into the mountain, and where we hiked up months later and recovered parts of the cockpit. I knew the path that runs along the skirt of the mountain that can't be seen from the road. I knew the grass that stood in tall waves and shimmers like an ocean when the moon is full, and I knew the snow that would eventually cover it all. Momentarily, all my aspirations of leaving this place and staying away scattered. To own a little piece of something on this earth, however insignificant , felt like the only thing in the world that I wanted.

After I shower now, I spend a long time standing naked in front of the mirror while I do my makeup and brush my hair, just going slow. Like any American girl, I learned early on that I should want my body to be something other than what it was. Not unfamiliar to most people, I spent years labeling it with symbols like L and 14, and later, XL and 16. I won't go into the details about what I wanted my body to be because whatever you are imagining is probably correct—skinnier, prettier, smarter. Doubtless, we each know the story so well from the view inside our own skin.

In the last few years, my body's needing and wanting to take a different form diminished, and friendship between my spirit and body has replaced that gnawing desire to be something else. When I started following "body positive" women on social media, I resisted what they said was beautiful. My eyes had been trained for so long to acknowledge a single standard that it took time to really believe the women who put up pictures of themselves in swimming suits—with folds in their skin, bellies that were not taut, and thighs that had no gap. It all took time to receive because, though I looked like these women, I had never called what I looked like beautiful. When I used words like "beautiful" to describe my own body, I almost felt that I was stealing something that wasn't mine. It took time and courage. It took a realignment of everything that I'd learned wasn't supposed to be mine. Over time I came to love my body, though—not just to say that I loved it, but to really love it and to know it like a dear friend.

Now I stand in front of the mirror, my stomach not flat, the wideness of my grandmother's hips written in my frame, my thighs with the muscles of my days playing soccer still barely visible, my breasts round like the two moons orbiting Jupiter. There are curves like a pencil line that I want to draw. It is all delicious to see, to know that she, this body, is mine. And perhaps, not so long down the road, this body will be the only one that I can confide in and know will understand me completely.

Thank You Letter

Teaching missionary lessons
I put my hand in a glove and
wiggled my fingers—
this is the body with the spirit.
To explain death,
I would take the glove off and move the hand
into the air, as if a spirit were rising
to heaven while the limp glove stayed
behind on the table.
The spirit, somehow shoved into taut skin,
hardly fitting. A restless, wise, curious light
and the body simply the dull keeper,
not the thing to love.
We closed the lesson, folded our arms to pray.
Walked two miles on a dirt road toward home
and stopped at the corner bakery for a pastry.
The sun was so hot I held bags of ice to my eyes.
Once, in that foreign country,
I was so sick I threw up every fifteen minutes for a whole
     day.
How is it I believed that my spirit would leave easily at
     death?
Convinced to betray such loyalty without first kissing
the soft skin on the inside of my arm?
Without running fingers along the skin of my thigh?
Without pressing my palms to the ocean of my stomach?

Without thanking my round hips profusely?
One last hand cupped full of my own breast?
Who's to say that when I die, my spirit won't fight like mad,
coil like an angry snake,
puff out big like a pufferfish,
stick out quills,
arch the back,
insist that my body come with.
My spirit reaching down, clawing the air, grasping,
all the way to heaven.

And I am not graceful about any of this some of the time. They say that part of grieving is to feel anger, and I haven't yet, at least not directly. The part of the earth that opened up when the news came to me is quiet, warm, and made of pastel colors. The sides are too steep to climb just yet. I don't know how to get out, or if I will ever find the way. Maybe anger rests just above the surface, and if I make my way to the top and reach over, I will be able to pull it down into my new world and shake it around until it turns into acceptance. Partly though, I just don't know who I would be angry at. Anger seems to want a destination, moving torpedo-like toward something particular, and since I don't believe that God orchestrates illness and hardship, I am too tired to hold onto a wily bit of anger on my own. So sadness, defiance, refusal, unwarranted optimism, gratitude, fear, joy, acceptance. These are the tools I have when I look to the future. I don't think they will fail me.

And what about God? My religious upbringing taught me the category of "trial"—a convenient box into which people place illness and disease. It often feels like your faithfulness and loyalty to God are on trial when something difficult happens. So many things are trials that it seems like we are all waiting in the side rooms to be called to the jury to see if we successfully navigated our devastating circumstances with grace and obedience. The flip side of believing in a God who orchestrates trials for "reasons," "for good," or "for growth," is that He will be with us every step of the journey, in the quiet moments when earthly support has faded and time has passed.

I have loved that idea, but now that my time for a "trial" has arrived, I cannot believe that God was behind it. In these moments, it feels most right to me to entirely bypass a male figure, the "He" we often speak of, and look towards a female god, or the divine female energy in the universe. The Divine Mother. It is a Mother that I need right now.

The first morning we were in Utah for Christmas break, we woke up to the smell of cinnamon rolls my mom had made for us before she went to work at the hospital. When my whole body ached from the steroids, my own mother drew a hot bath with lavender and a candle on the ledge, and she folded my laundry and tucked a soft blanket around me in the early mornings. This is what mothers do, and it is what my soul searches for as well as my body. I also felt my dad's kindness when he hugged me, hesitant sometimes, but clearly making an effort toward tenderness. I sensed his determination to somehow heal me when he made me spinach and protein shakes every morning.

In my moment of trial, I am most interested in imagining female gods and female ancestors, and Mother Earth herself getting the news right along with me. She must have set to work weaving an earthly net to catch me. She is the bird whose wing I am under. She has not told me what I should learn here, has not asked for my obedience in exchange for her love, has not given credence to my thoughts about how maybe this trial is supposed to make me humble. In truth, I don't think a male God actually asks any of these things either, but because we are vulnerable, we need Him to be powerful. We need someone able to cure and change what should be incurable and unchangeable, so we give this work to Him.

In the religion I know most intimately, I never heard mention of a Divine Female until I was in college, and even then, it felt blasphemous to say aloud. I had never considered Her or Her work. I'd talked about Her so little that she had no job, and no expectations, in my religious world view. When I finally began to imagine Her, I saw a wide open sky of possibilities. A Divine Mother could be anything, could do anything, that I needed Her to be and do. So now She sits quietly with me, Her spirit as calm as a forest, and holds me, warm and close under her swan-like wing, the feathers sturdy and imperfect, discolored in places, but determined to hold me safe until the storm passes.

Just Before Things Changed, a poem

The woman who lost her husband of fifty-seven years is gardening to keep her mind off things when we walk by. Yesterday, I felt a pang of loneliness while mixing the cookie dough. It was unwarranted—I have everything. But it fluttered around still, looking to take flight. Two children climbing a tree in the front yard, one napping in her crib, her arm around the soft, white bear. The woman who is gardening and gardening is not like me, and is. The wisteria will bloom for us regardless, the snap peas will continue their wild ascent, the waves down at the ocean will tumble and polish everything they wash up against. We will blow out birthday candles and wonder who it is we could have been. But we are here now, both of us, and all the people in between. The world is as lonely as a snowy egret out on the swampy water, and as tender as the running of sandpipers following the water in and out, their feet barely making prints in the sand. Here we are in it, our hands in the dirt, planting seeds for the future, baking warm cookies for children when they decide to come in.

Everything looks different and exactly the same. It is okay to grasp back to what is no longer there. It is okay to look forward with fear. Everything is rolling ahead now, almost steadily, as if I got on a rollercoaster and headed up the first hill. I brace the best I can and throw my hands in the air, waving to my kids down below to assure them it's all supposed to happen this way, because what else can I do?

I always thought that my parents were an entity that created my world and orbited it while I was a child and a teenager. I thought this meant that they knew everything, even on until the end. I did not realize that we would both soon arrive at the two bookends of adulthood with an air of knowing grace and mercy for one another. I didn't anticipate this arrival. How could I have? Me looking out across a landscape that my two parents had just finished crossing, and them looking back as I begin.

My mom and I are exactly thirty years apart, which always seemed like a very long time, until I turned thirty and realized that, from there on out, I would be crossing ground with her footsteps always just in front of me. She was a mother of young children in her thirties as I am now. The time she sat in front of the utility building in the car and cried when I was very young because we didn't have money for the bill had always plagued and confused me, but now that our worlds have intersected, it does not. Of course she had reason to cry, because it is hard to be old enough that the world expects you to have it all together but still young enough that you know you don't.

My mom and dad's inherent wise-ness—which in part must be a gift of age—has shown me that even they know that space under the wing so well. I think back and feel sure there must have been moments when we were driving together in the car, or walking through the neighborhood, or eating breakfast quietly, when they must have tried to tell me, or at least wanted to tell me what it was like to spend time under the wing. Even when their children were were riding up top, it was clear that we were still naive about the sting of living.

In the midst of what can't be known about this diagnosis, I sat in the basement of the house I grew up in as a teenager and sorted out my thoughts. More than once, my dad put his rough hands on my shoulders and pulled me in close without saying anything when I came upstairs after writing. And my mom washed our clothes, made us dinner, changed the sheets, and bathed my children with a fervency that only comes about when one truly believes they are doing the work of healing.

One bitter cold day, Carl and I and the three kids, got in our minivan with my parents and drove south, far enough beyond the city that we felt like outsiders. We saw a group of people riding horses through a snowy field. We stopped at the church properties my dad takes care of in the summers. He pointed out the fence where a vine grows over and he ate the grapes while he worked in the hot sun. They bought us ice cream at Dairy Queen where half the booths were filled with men in cowboy hats and their white-haired wives. We stopped a mile from their home at a hill, and my children sledded while my dad took video after video on his phone of my children zooming down the mountain on the long, red, plastic sled they had bought in anticipation of our arrival.

Being taken care of in this way acknowledges, without directly addressing the problem, and it keeps me moving forward, following curiously their footsteps which sometimes wind for no reason or stop at dead ends. I want to ask my parents just how and when they learned to heal their children this way. What is it I need to know? I don't think they would answer; they would just hand me a warm taco and a handful of M&M's and give me a seat on the couch while we listened to some old records, the snow falling endlessly beyond the windows.

One afternoon, the kids and I hiked up behind my parent's house into the mountains I know so well. It was bitter cold and clear. The top layer of snow was as abundant and light as freshly dumped glitter. I know this because I, too, have had whole bottles of glitter dumped on my floor. Our snow boots crunched through as we forged up the hillside.

We were not in a hurry because we were not actually going anywhere. On our way up a trail, Remy was the first one to get distracted with the thought of sliding down the steep dirt embankment on his belly. He, of course, was delighted to find that his clothes were thick enough, and the snow slick enough, that he flew down the hill. I was anything but graceful, but it felt important for my kids to know that I would follow them. I knew that my kids knew nothing of what had changed for me. I knew they only saw what was in front of them, and in that moment, what was in front of them was simply their mom. An image that has somehow caused them to believe that there is someone who knows how to do everything—match and ball the socks, make the perfect chocolate chip cookie, and sing just long enough that they fall asleep before there is silence.

Every hour or so I still got the icy feeling down the left side of my body, starting with my eye and running down through my hand. I felt it at the top of the hill, but it did not stop me from going headfirst down that snowy embankment just before sunset. Out there on that glittery foothill, sledding on the underskirt of the mountains girthy dress, pulled across the wide hips of that familiar body, my illness was anonymous. No one knew that the vision in my right eye was blurred, my synapses couldn't quite make the connection, and misfired down the left side of my body. The secrecy of those facts was a comfort, and for the first time since the diagnosis I forgot what had transpired, forgot that prayers were floating on the air for me from all directions. I ducked below them all and slid again down the snowy hill, my children standing at the top and laughing in disbelief.

From Here on Out

For seven years I kept my children from the darkness.

They knew light blues of morning,

the kick of their shoe on the pavement as they ride their
bikes to school.

Digging their hands into sun-warmed dirt of the afternoon
garden.

Light skimming down the branches on a mud-packed trail.

Their mother's face in the afternoon before dinner,

sometimes tired, or at peace, full with a hundred things she
will never say.

Each night they bathed, saw that the light through the
windows was no longer light,

A book before bed, please keep the closet light on, sometimes nightmares and they are standing at the edge of
my bed looking for an escape

from the darkness in the warm, soft mountain of my body.

But last night my daughter and I sat in the front yard
  beneath a navy sky.
Stars like paperclip-poked holes did not make the night
  bright.
When we had settled she heard owls, bats, raccoons.
The night was ordinary. Not even a moon.
I felt her breathing in the dark, her body slowing like the
  flowers that had already closed.
It was all new to her.
And I was sorry that in order to protect
I'd kept them from the dark these many years.

I know Carl stays up late some nights after I'm asleep, reading the academic papers on the disease that he downloaded before he graduated and lost access to the massive research databases of Stanford University Library. I know he knows more than he is telling me. Sometimes I turn over in bed, and he is up, the glow of words on the computer reflected back on his face. I am still too scared to ask what he's found out, and I think he's still too scared to tell me. Anyone who hears the news seems to be aptly devastated, empathetic, and aware of how life-altering this all is—and part of me wants to ask them why, what do they know that I don't? I want them to explain to me why they are sad to hear the news. I want them to offer up the experiences and secrets they know. I want them to do the work I'm not yet willing to do.

I am surprised by the way I need people to resolve this part of the equation for me. I imagine the people around me, the ones who told me they researched it after I'd told them the news. I imagine them in a circle, holding onto the handle of a giant colorful parachute, like the one we used on the grassy field in elementary school. I am lying flat on my back in the middle while the people on the outside pump their arms up and down until the fabric is high enough that air fills the inside and everyone pulls inward, sitting on the edge of the fabric. I remember that feeling so well; we had created something so magical, an impenetrable temporary world that no one on the outside could experience. I remember feeling giddy about how the colors cast an otherworldly glow inside the parachute bubble, how the air held everything up, even when we couldn't see it.

I've always been a passionate lover of color, and there was something so satisfying about my world being changed so briefly under that giant parachute—the thin swaths of fabric our sky, the grass our terrain, all of us survivors in a new place. I feel that same curiosity and awareness now. Only I am not doing the work that feels too hard to take on. I am not moving the parachute up and down against gravity, against the thick air. I am just lying there, looking up. This seems like a great effort and all for me, I note, but when I look at the faces around the circle working fervently, they do not seem perplexed; they seem purposeful and unresentful in doing the work I cannot do for now. I feel the warm grass along my shoulder blades, this new sky with slices of orange, red, blue, and purple moving so near that it almost touches my face, and then up again. Always the light streaming through, making everything brilliant and bearable.

I, perhaps impulsively, reached out to one of most creative people I know, a friend who is now well-known photographer and teacher. I knew her from college, and we both knew loved each other in youngness and naivety. I sensed a kinship with her and with her relationship to tension, a healthy regard for the unknown, a similar curiosity in what tangible objects unexpected change can create. In her gentleness, she responded to me, even when I knew she was busy. On an icy afternoon I found myself in Diana's living room.

The golden hour was about to stream in through her windows overlooking the city I grew up in. She was not in a hurry, even though the sunlight would soon be gone. She kneeled in front of me on the teal carpet and asked me what it felt like. I told her about the bird, the wing I had once and for so long stood upon, and how, in one fell swoop, I had climbed down under the warm wing. She nodded. I knew she understood what I was talking about because I know that, in her own ways, she has lived there too, has photographed the world from under the wing. In speaking to her I realized that I don't want this ache to be just one thing. And I don't want to be its only keeper.

As the sun's golden light spread across my pastel polka dot dress—the one I found at a second hand store in Sweden, and the one I chose to wear because I have a photograph I love of myself from that time years ago holding Thea's hand as she learned to walk—she took the first few photographs. I had been drawn to the dress because it flowed over my body without allowing anyone to actually see my body. I loved the colors, and I loved that it had likely been worn by some older woman in Sweden before me. Maybe it was even the ghost of a dress one of my ancestors wore. We took the first photographs while Carl played with the kids outside.

I had asked this friend specifically to photograph me without clothes. I was nervous, but I knew I trusted her to do it, and I knew that my body, perhaps also already giving in to some of the sorrow, had been the one to ask.

We moved from the living room to her bedroom, her bed still unmade. She left the room, and I unzipped the dress, letting it fall to the floor. I could hear my children playing in the snow with Carl through the bedroom window. I could hear her children talking to each other in the living room. We were not alone; everything was in motion around us. A parent is not uninterrupted in sorrow, joy, or creativity. The improvisation stems from limited time to understand and process it all. These restraints propel the work.

I stood in front of her bedroom wall, my shadow like a curved and curious shape behind me. I was no longer nervous when she came back in the room, my clothes in a pile, and I was not nervous when she put the lens to her eye, or even when I heard the click of the film moving through the roll. My image, this conflicted moment, imprinted itself inside that small box. I saw Hilde totter along the back patio behind Carl; Diana's daughter came in the room and did not seem surprised to see me there without clothes. "What are you doing?" she asked. "We are artists," Diana answered. This was a moment that could not be made alone; it needed both of us, or more accurately, all eight of us at the house that day.

I stood, looking forward, the scar from a tumor, once removed, still thick down my middle, and the smile of three c-sections hanging like a hammock between my hip bones. I find that this same scar looks and means different things to me on different days. Everything full, the flesh perhaps fuller than it's ever been. I don't know what it looked like from my friend's photo lens, but she kept saying, "beautiful!", and every part of me wanted to believe her, wanted my body to stay just the way that it was at that moment.

Nothing stays the same. The future is sometimes grieved for what it might be; the past is sometimes grieved for what might have been, but for that hour everything was golden. I felt that I understood more clearly than I ever had what it must be like to be in bloom, to unfurl in the thaw of spring, to look around and see the world opening, unsure of what is coming, but showing up nonetheless.

I think of Mary Oliver and the sadness of her childhood, how she wandered away from her home for hours to roam the landscape. Mother nature showed up for her and then sustained her life and work. I think of Annie Dillard, when I first read her books in high school and saw that she relied on what she saw outside to guide her writing. I felt like maybe there was a place for me after all. I am not Mary Oliver, or Annie Dillard, but nature is not discerning about who it shares its secrets with. Nature has always meant solace for me. It has always yielded answers when I had none, given unceasingly.

On the drive back to California the snow was too deep through the Sierra's, so we took a detour. We drove directly into Death Valley and followed the signs to the lowest point in all of North America. We parked, bundled up, and walked alongside a hundred tourists down a white sand highway a mile out to the salt flats. Remy thought he would run to the other side when we finally reached the end of the path. "To Mars!" he said. He ran straight for five minutes until he looked like a black dot out on the infinite white. He came back when he realized he would never make it to other side.

The world from here looks so much smaller than it actually is. Time is as wide as those salt flats. On our way into the park we saw a coyote on the road. It seemed shy, like it was tricking us into thinking that it didn't know how to survive in one of the harshest environments on earth. I mistook it for a red fox even though, upon reflection, it clearly was not. I wanted very much to take the red fox for a sign that everything would be all right because red foxes have shown up in other places for me before. This scared coyote though? I did not know what to make of her, except that, when we came back through, the coyote was gone, and I didn't wonder for a moment if she would survive. I knew she would. I knew that somewhere out there, to some warm and undiscoverable spot, she returned each night, gathering to face the day again in the morning.

Normal life resumed. I ran errands in the rain with the kids. They fought in the back of the car. I had to pick up the radiologist's report and the disc with my MRI images on it and bring them to another doctor. I left my kids in the car because the office was about to close, and I couldn't make it across the parking lot in time with all three of them. The sky was grey and low, and I ran in my yellow rain boots, even through a puddle. Thea wanted a popsicle so fervently, and I had told her that we would go and find one just as soon as this errand was done. I needed the reports for my doctor's visit in the coming week, but it also felt important, even imperative, to hold them, to have some proof of everything doctors had told me.

I recognized the woman in radiology by the same accent she'd had on the phone earlier that day. She was as kind as I imagined she would be, and it was nice to be able to look her in the eyes and thank her in person. It was an exchange that felt all too normal for the information she pushed in an envelope across the counter into my hands—a few lines typed on a piece of paper that dictated a part of my story that I had not asked to live. This is life; it seems funny to me now that I ever imagined I would walk through it unscathed. I took the envelope and ran back out to the car.

My daughter was eager to get going, but I sat in the driver's seat and opened the smooth envelope as if it were a gift or a letter from an old friend. In the back of my mind, I thought that I would open it and find that somebody had misread, had been mistaken, had not meant to use those words, but there it was at the end of the report in the final synopsis,: unmistakably those words, without apology or hesitation.

I read over the results, now a little more familiar with the medical terminology, making my high school anatomy class feel really useful. Of course my deliberateness was just an interruption to what Thea thought the errand was for. She wanted a popsicle and wiggled around in the backseat feeling the urgency of her request. I folded the papers carefully and placed them back alongside the disc of images. I looked back at her, so impatient, never full, a tiny manifestation of I what I had imagined for so long that the world was—something for me to grasp, understand, own, command, serve.

The papers with my diagnosis felt a like manifestation of something else, a reminder that life—even when it is ungraspable, misunderstood, un-owned, not interested in our service—is vibrant in unexpected ways. We went to get the popsicles at a health food store nearby, Thea and Hilde talking the whole way with sounds and words that I couldn't even discern. Even though it is the furthest thing from the truth, I can't help but think "What if this is the last time I am able to do this thing with my children?" I am compelled to infuse each experience with the weight of the possibility that it will not occur again. However untrue, however unsustainable I know this to be, I wonder how long this magic will last.

I was back in the optometry office. The little Christmas tree with the blinking lights was now packed in a cardboard box in some closet, new people were sitting in the soft padded chairs, the same window had the same slatted blinds. If I could have looked over the houses and trees, I would have seen the ocean.

My double vision was almost gone, and I saw just one of everything again. I sat again with my chin rested on a contraption while a different doctor, a neurology specialist, looked into my eyes. The common thread of these fragile first weeks is that people have been kind, and this new doctor was no different. He said that he knew about me from Dr. Chavez. Optometrists see sixth nerve palsies every day, but I was young and healthy and new to this, so they suspected either a brain tumor or MS. He said that he knew something was wrong after hearing Dr. Chavez speak on the phone that morning because a specialist like himself is only called if something needs immediate attention. I picture then-me ,who knew none of this, sitting out in the waiting room, and the now-me. It feels like I have passed through a dark glass wall. What I thought I knew were not the things that are.

How do we close that distance and make sense of what we thought we knew and what we actually do? I think of my daughter once asking just before falling asleep, "Mom, what is on the other side of a black hole?" To which I answered "nothing," because I simply could not make up an answer on the spot. But maybe this is it. Maybe there is not a plan for these things. Maybe God simply was not concerned that I was down here, blurry eyed, with a diagnosis that will potentially change my life.

Maybe Albert Camus's condemned man in *The Stranger* was right, saying "I looked up at the mass of signs and stars in the night sky and laid myself open for the first time to the benign indifference of the world." For the work I have done, benign indifference seems a generous offering. It's not that God is not intimate. Maybe it's just that my suffering is so small in comparison, the people in the world so capable of caring for me, that He doesn't need to get involved. Maybe it's that we are all going to die, our bodies the only maps that really know the way back. And maybe God just thinks, "I will see you when you get here. I don't want to pluck you from the sadness. The earth will cradle you. The world will show up more vibrantly."

Just a mile from my home, the waves in the ocean seem like they are trying to pull themselves doggedly up and out of this place. The earth is gulping in the winter rain, day after day, as if it were the last chance to drink. Thea's curls are a miracle of chance. She paints a dog who, for some reason, is speaking the words, "It's in the backyard." The birthday cakes were made by someone who took the time. Hilde grabs my hand and says "C'mon," as she leads me to the basket of books that she wants me to read. Remy, who shoots baskets with a dull ball in the street, is not deterred by the number of airballs he sends up.

I think of the random people whose lives have recently brushed up against mine: the grandmother of a boy in my daughter's kindergarten class who told me in Spanish that she doesn't go out much, just to work at the hotel downtown and to go to the market on the bus, because everything is still new and scary here; the people at the downtown Veteran's Christmas charity dinner that I served at, and my service was so stupid because I stood in the back while they ate when something in me was saying I should go talk with them; the doctor this morning who told me I would live a good life, that I would see the world and myself differently because of this disease. And I believed his blessing, as if he were God speaking to me.

A Big Question

The nightlight sent dim stars into the corners of the room,
"Mom, will you ever leave me?" Of course not. My daughter breathing in sleep, exhaling into the darkness.

What is the opposite of grief?

My daughter's birthday party—
Rainbow cake shaped like a unicorn and twenty kids
    singing to her,
the melody rising into the trees above.
A hidden lake in the high Uintas. The hawk perched on the
    jungle gym early in the morning,
diving slightly into the wet grass. A plane full of strangers
    singing to a woman on her 91st birthday, the stewardess
    placing a crown of pretzels on her thin, curly hair.

My daughter used only water to paint on a paper.
She held the paper to the lighted window,
as it dried and the marks disappeared,
she said, "I painted God."

After the popsicles that day we went to Taco Bell, where the lighting inside was a strange green and orange from the counters and the overhead shelves of tortillas and cheese. There was a loud dinging sound that did not stop for five minutes, and when it finally did, the two female employees and I looked at each other and nodded in relief. I watched them make the three burritos for my children, and again—and perhaps because everything feels this way when the ground shifts under you—it felt like an act of grace. While I stood there and watched I was confronted with another aspect of all this, one that is far too complicated for an answer, but still worth facing head on.

I couldn't help but think, "What if one of these women working at Taco Bell had been diagnosed with the same thing as me? Would the world open for her in the same way? Would nets be woven to catch them? Would the space under the wing open to them as immediately as it did for me? I believe that the powers that do not belong to this earth would care for them as much as anyone else, but would they have the support I do earthside? Would they have the means to be able to buy ingredients at a natural foods store in some attempt to keep change at bay? Would they have access to insurance and doctors and treatments in the same way I do? The likely answer is no. Santa Cruz, where I live, is full of people recently immigrated from Mexico and Central America and considering by my inability to navigate healthcare systems, I can't imagine doing it in a language that is not my own.

My disease is here as an unwelcome guest who has unpacked her bags and is setting up house in the spare bedroom. But I do not have to host her alone. I do not have to face her on my own, almost ever. And that fact is a privilege. It speaks to my privilege. It is not something I'm proud of, but also not something I am willing to give up entirely because I am scared still of what that would mean.

I was so tired the afternoon I picked up my MRI images. After the kids were in bed that night, Carl and I sat in our bed, the bedframe from craigslist, the mattress a hand-me-down from a neighbor's little girl's room who never slept on it. The cheap pillows, the heavy blue blanket, the one that was in the trunk that my grandma kept behind the couch, the one I coveted always, was on us. It is torn now, revealing not batting but some other ancestral pattern, faded pink and orange flowers on soft cream fabric—like maybe the quilt was sewn multiple times, one on top of the other instead of just starting over. I wonder if its unusual heaviness comes from this re-sew-ing, re-giving, re-doing in our own way.

The rain was heavy outside our window, the muddy yard chewed up by the dog, the rat we would later catch in a trap probably burrowing in for the winter, though we couldn't hear her below our floorboards yet. We uploaded the disc's images to my laptop and waited while the computer buzzed, processing the information, the fuzzy grey mass of my brain. The occipital views, the front lobes, the brain stem, the tender part at the back of my neck. And then they appeared, at least two dozen images arranged in little squares. I searched through them as if I were looking at the images from the Hubble telescope. Both sets of pictures so familiar, so much like home, and yet completely foreign, so far away.

The unexpected anthem of the Hubble telescope advent calendar had followed me all month; it was not just an apparition on the sleepless night of my diagnosis. NASA released one image a day, and each day I called my kids to the computer to see., I wanted them to marvel at their inability to comprehend what is out there, some thousands of light years away, but although they liked the pictures, they could quite recognize the impossibility of understanding. Of course neon rainbows flashed out of blackness. Of course thousands of stars congregated like confetti after a celebration. Of course a nebula glows in the dark. They believe all this as easily as they imagine the see-through fish that must live at the bottom of the Mariana Trench.

Stretching the imagination comes naturally to us. But here, with these images of my own brain in front of me, I could not stretch my own imagination far enough to believe those eerie white spots so clear among the grey matter really did belong to me. I could see the spots clearly, like stars in a dark sky scattered across my cortex—one near the brain stem, the one they thought could have been a brain tumor before it was imaged, the one that stopped the muscle in my right eye from being able to move to the side, creating double vision which I had soon learned was a classic symptom. How did I not know? How did I not understand what to look for before it was declared mine? A new constellation. It all seems so obvious now.

The intimacy of sharing these images felt as familiar as the three separate weeks over the past eight years that Carl and spent in hospital rooms after our children were born. Romance condensed into an understanding that, whatever this was would be ours. Even though I imagine that he felt as alone as I did, there was something intimate about that attempt to claim something as ours. I put my head on his shoulder while we looked at my brain, and we discovered together the places we could point to. The millimeters of white signaled another beginning for us. The whiteness was only visible because the contrast dye the MRI techs sent through my IV had seeped through the blood-brain barrier and lit up the offending passages like a constellation that will guide us from now on, all this knowledge and unknowing, contained here, right in my head.

Change happened in the flick of an instant and pierced the part of me that truly believed I was impervious to hardship. The hole it left did not seal itself back up, but rather made apparent and very real the impermanence of all things. I could not seal the hole and un-see what I'd witnessed. I don't know that I'd want to.

On the phone with my dad. Just before we hung up, he told me that he accidentally told his sister, my aunt, about my diagnosis while they were at lunch. I told him it was fine, that I would rather other people do the telling sometimes. I don't want to be there feeling like I have to cushion the shock of the news by stumbling quickly ahead with optimism and reassurance that it won't be that bad. It's nice for people to get the news ahead of time, with space to process a line or two, time to send up a prayer, light a candle, do a bit of research.

What my dad said next, though, surprised me. He said he was sorry to have shared the news because, really, it was something I could potentially keep to myself, keep secret, even for years. I think he meant to comfort me, not put pressure on me, as an act of courage in being willing to hold my secret with me.

I started thinking again about the first moments in the ER when the nurse I can't remember in detail delivered the news so plainly in that small windowed room. I was full of drugs, head aching, and nauseated, and at the end of her sentence I cried one muffled, ugly-faced cry, that I still wish I could have suppressed. That was it, no more than ten minutes. So brief; everything was different, yet when I looked up it all was the same—all the wires, the nurse standing at his station outside the door, the dimming light through the blinds.

Carl was there then and now, his presence like a meadow. I felt him lift the weight of the news and place it somewhere beyond my reach. But still, I wanted to tell someone, lots of someones; I didn't want to carry this alone. It was then that I knelt on the wing of the bird as she glided softly to the ground. It was then that I pictured myself sliding to the ground with the grace that I want so badly to have. I pictured my feet hitting the ground as I looked around deftly and ducked under the feathers into the warmth below.

It is in this space that I imagine looking around and seeing the people from my life who knew sadness and loss long before I did. It was from here that I began frantically texting a few close friends, my mother-in-law, my parents, my sisters. Maybe it was wrong to thrust the weight of the burden from me and ask others to drop everything to pick it up, but I don't have a list of rules to follow when the path I was following veered so quickly into new territory. Unsurprisingly, the people I reached out to showed up immediately and began unrolling their nets to catch me in whatever way I might fall.

And when I was done texting back and forth with people, I finally looked up and saw that everyone in the clear, pinkish light, everyone in the safe cave of that wing, was ready for me, ready to teach me what they'd learned and known for longer than I had even known what I didn't know. Their eyes were deep with experience. Some looked defeated and sad. I looked around and saw wise, gentle, empathetic faces looking back at me—and also a clarity that sometimes things do not turn out okay. Sometimes there aren't answers, reasons, lessons. I took a step forward and realized that I was not ready. I stumbled, and the people there came forward and caught me. I knew then that I would be okay, that sometimes home looks different than what you thought you were moving toward.

My symptoms are gone. The left side of my body is not going numb, and the vision in my right eye is no longer distorted. At the beach yesterday, Thea found a long rope of seaweed, and Carl and I turned it while she jumped in the sand. I did not think about being sick in the future. I am fortunate that, most of the time, I am not. I don't even know what images and ideas to tether myself to, and even if I did, they likely wouldn't be the right ones. Nothing is what I could have predicted.

Last summer I was at the local swimming pool with my kids, and I saw a man from my church. I've known him since I was twelve years old and have also always known that he has MS. It seemed to always be something people said in whispers and with concern. He was swimming laps across the long blue pool. I must have been curious because I kept looking toward him until he was done. I don't remember the details, but I do remember that he seemed to do most of the work with his arms. I'd only seen him at church in long church pants, so seeing his legs wet and disobedient felt intrusive. I couldn't look away, though; it was surprisingly beautiful to watch these few moments of what I determined to be bravery and doggedness. It felt like a miracle, almost biblical. He lifted his body up out of the water and up the ladder with the strength of his arms. I looked away from him to help one of my kids, and when I looked back, he was moving across the cement with his walker, a towel across his shoulders.

I see now, even I knew it a little then, that it wasn't my place to award him with words like "brave" because, even if he was, I was not qualified to evaluate his character or endow his activities with a significance that made me feel better.

It is strange to think that it may someday be me pulling myself mightily from a swimming pool. I will not be the spectator. I will be the doer. I like to be a navigator of my own way, the keeper of my feelings.

The unknowns feel like a challenge, which interests me and makes me wonder what it is like to be at the center of a hardship. Is it that I want people to watch me? Is my ego so determined to believe that anyone will actually see?

I wonder what synapses are not firing readily enough. I wonder if a relapse is around the corner. Last night I woke up with a head full of panic. I could not deflect the swirling mass, I could not get the thoughts to move around, up, or over. I just lay there in the dark, a microwave light on down the hall, the raccoons finally not scratching at the fence in the backyard—what could they be doing out there? What little thing could their hands be scratching at?

My body feels like a stranger to me these days, like it has gone off in the night and told me not to follow. It is secretive, de-myleanating without my knowledge. It keeps me guessing what will come next, which part of my body will momentarily cease to function. At the same time, this body has settled into itself and has become comfortable in its own skin. I want to believe that it won't betray me, I want to believe it will listen to my stern voice when I say "no more. You cannot do this anymore."

People I saw, or thought I saw, under the wing

The woman from the playground at my children's school. I don't know her name, but she held my daughter up on the monkey bars when I was busy chasing my toddler on the other side of the playground. I gave her a Christmas gift wrapped in purple paper. Something about her cheerful "Hi Ashley!", with so much sincere connection the morning we got back from Christmas break, made me believe that my suspicions were true, that she did know hardship in ways that I did not. She turns the jump rope for all the kids for a full half hour some afternoons. She once told me about a large house that she cleaned on the west side of town and how she is not from here, but from the east coast. Maybe I'm wrong, but in some ways I hope that I'm not. She is the kind of person that I want to be there each time I duck down under the safety of that wing.

The man from school who rides a blue bicycle to school with his granddaughter each morning. I also don't know his name or if it is better to greet him in English or Spanish, but on the afternoon after I gave him a Christmas present, he came over to me while I was on the phone making my first appointment with the eye doctor and pressed three small boxes into my palm. "Para usted," he said, and rode away on his bicycle. I smiled, and when I got off the phone, I looked at what he'd given me. Three pocket mirrors. One with birds on the cover, one with the famous red-bandana-ed woman saying "We can do it!", and one with unicorns, which Thea loved. I've thought a lot about those three mirrors and what they must mean as the opening gift to this journey, and still I don't know.

What I do know, though, is that they were given by a man who is not living in his native country. A man who in some earlier life was very handsome and young. I don't know what has been hard in his life, and I likely never will, but I like to think of him as the gatekeeper to that place under the wing that we will likely all climb down under at some point. I picture him there pressing the best gifts he has into the palms of people who don't yet know that they are about to experience something that will be different than anything they have ever encountered.

There is an older man who works every day in Thea's kindergarten class. The weekly announcement note I found in her backpack said that he is part of a foster grandparent program. One time we were walking along a busy road, and he rode by on his bicycle and yelled, "Hi Thea!" as he passed. I didn't recognize him, but Thea immediately did and couldn't believe that he had recognized her. When I drop her off at school each morning, I see him sitting at the back of the classroom, a black beanie on, putting papers in folders, writing "Good job!" on kindergarten drawings.

The pretty woman at the dinner party. Gold earrings and perfect hair that sweeps back in a way that mine never will. I know that her husband died of cancer just before Thanksgiving, but I don't know her well enough to say anything useful. I notice her scarf—it is so pretty, bunched around her neck, the gray fabric, the little diamond rimmed with gold pin that holds it all together. I want to tell her how pretty she is, but it feels so dumb.

The woman at the ER in the orange scrubs who gave me the stuffed giraffe on that very first day. No doubt she is there under the wing. How else would she have known that the right thing to do in that moment was to take my hospital bill to the shredder. She must have known from experience that there is a time to sit alone with grief and let it fully clothe you. She must have had some sense of the sacredness of those hours between getting my diagnosis and returning to my front door, right back into the life that was mine before. She must have known that I needed those hours before life returned to me at full speed. I will always be grateful to her, a stranger, for that.

My sister-in-law is also there under the wing. I regret that I did not ask her more when she was diagnosed with this same disease two years ago. I want to say that nervousness inhibited me, and I think that is partly true, but also blind selfishness—the comfort that comes from keeping myself distant from what is hard in another person's life. Even someone who is otherwise close. I think that I wanted to take her at her word when she said she was okay, when she showed that she was fine, strong, un-interrupted. I know now that is not true. No person who is thrown something difficult is un-interrupted.

I have beginnings that define the record of my life. When I think back on the birth of my three children, I realize that shocking newness can never be replicated no matter how much I wish it could. Those first five days in a hospital room, like we'd both been born into a soft nest. The edges of the rest of the world blurred to colors without shape. My pain brought a clarity that I wouldn't trade for anything. Those first laps around the hospital wing after my c-sections and two surgeries were the slowest my body has ever been, and I felt so proud about what I'd done. When I look back, I am still proud.

Even in those first moments after receiving the news in the hospital room, an image came to me and unfolded itself as a swift movement, as if I were watching myself. I pictured a great bird with strong, wide wings—like the swans that lived on the lake by our house in Sweden, on the tiny beach I visited in the afternoons with my two small children when I was unsure how to do anything else. The image of those swans has stuck with me; they were bigger in real life than I thought they would be. I marvelled at the way they pulled themselves up into the air so fiercely and then moved their great wings with grace. I'd see them land across the water on a little island full of untouched weeds that burst through the warm ground of Spring.

When I got the news, I pictured one of those birds, only bigger, and I pictured myself sitting atop, confident in both my own ability and in the ability of the world to fulfill everything I had always expected. When the nurse came in the room and, without even closing the door, told me what the neurologist had seen in my brain, I also saw in my mind the great swan circle through the sky and land over on the island. I saw a scared and brave me slide down the wing and climb underneath. The place itself perhaps knew that I would show up long before I arrived. Parts of this space feel shadowy and unknown, holding the defeat and sadness that might someday be mine to tell. But in this entryway, at the beginning of things, I don't know what to expect.

The point, though, is not my diagnosis, my future, or my desire for sympathy. The point is that we all have something: either it was there, is there, or will be there. We will all have something that will change our lives within minutes. We may think that we know exactly how our tapestry will turn out as we attach the warps to the top of the loom. We do this work of pulling taut the threads, the work we are able to control, the best that we can. But at some point, the weft will be something different than we imagined. We will weave our threads through the long pieces we first put in place, and a new pattern will appear—a distinct, pointable layer where everything has shifted. I don't think this is the only time my tapestry will change, but for now, as I pull each thread across, I can see I am creating something different than I set out to make. I am utterly compelled by the process—it calls for me to be my most creative self.

I am entering into a different world with new rules. I know so little about the changes I am looking at. Parts of it seem to contain sadness I don't want to touch, but I also want to believe that there are bright, unknown colors in what lies on the other side of conclusives, of endings, of beginnings, of what seems impossible to take on.

And so it seems with all of this, a beginning. A time of newness. Part of this beginning is sad, but that sadness is paralleled with something vibrant. Something vital. This is an experiment, nothing more. An experiment, an attempt to capture, to pin down some of what transpired when, not for the first time in my life, the world shifted just enough to let me in. I can do nothing more than attempt to better understand what it is to hurt, so that I can better understand what it is to heal. So many people are here, under that wing, living lives that are beautiful in spite of pain. And some lives, I now see, are simply hard.

I don't know what will be required of me. But I do know—like the yellow flowers that bloomed on the bushes in our front yard, or like the deep snow I walked through in the mountains with my children, or the full moon that stretched across the bay as we drove home late one night and listened to the same music my parents used to play for me on long drives—I do know that the world is rich with carved-out spaces that will take me in. I believe that refuge can function beyond geography. My storm so far has been meager, but real. This newness, this beginning, my own. There are a hundred ways to believe this.

Epilogue

Even after all this, I am not always that nice. Sometimes I look at my kids and think, "who are you to bully me this way?" To take all my time, and my secret ice cream stash, and still forget to say "thank you." Who are you to not understand the ways my world changed so recently? I know that none of this is theirs to carry yet. Their hearts, too, will know what it can carry when the heaviness arrives. Even in these moments when I recognize that even their presence is what cares for me, I am all selfish, an oyster with a pearl of selfishness at the center. I just want silence, to read a book, to write in the kitchen alone. But this morning I looked at my children in the driveway. Thea's hair was a forest of wild curls, the braids I did poorly because I don't know another way, and that she then slept on. Her wide, beautiful forehead, the hair blowing across it in the breeze. To one side of us were the retreating storm clouds from the night before, Heading out across the ocean to cause some ruckus we would not know. To the other side was the brightness of morning lights. Remy, in his green rain boots and the haircut I gave him, one longer strand still sticking up over his ear. Hilde, a perfect creature that believes the succulents keep living despite our neglect, just for her.

The light on my children, and I can't stress this enough, was like snow, like moonbeams, like foam at the ocean—a brightness that made me remember that these three human beings are people I am madly in love with. I didn't say it, just stood there, their dumb mom, the one they know everything and nothing about, taking it all in. We walked to school along the sidewalk, the tiny red-purple flowers still in bloom on that wiry bush next to the lavender. Thea held my hand, Hilde on the other side. They stopped to look at worms in the gutter, and Remy remembered the one as long as his arm that he found in Sweden, which did not, in fact ever happen, but I did not say that. And then we were in the parking lot, and the school bell rang, and I heard Thea say, "Mom, wait for me!" some ways behind. I looked back and didn't see her. Then I did. She was stooped to the asphalt in the same place she stops every day on the walk home from school. Someone must have broken a bracelet or necklace near there, because she never ceases to find a small bead, a shell, or a polished stone with a hole through the middle that she gathers in her hand. I could not hurry her; it seemed irreverent, with the light still that way falling down and all over us. The kids and parents were walking past her into the school. I know she heard the bell, but she continued collecting, and made her way to me.

Just outside her classroom, the children already sitting at their spot on the carpet, she bent down again in front of a puddle and tossed one of the tiny shells into it. "Look, mom! It's a magic shell! Do you see the way it changes color in the water?" At first I didn't see it, but the harder I looked, the closer I got to the ground, I saw it, I swear I did. A magic shell changing color right before my eyes.

Acknowledgments

I want to thank the circle of people who made this book possible in such a short period of time. Blair Hodges, who I was lucky enough to work with again. Michael Austin, who believes in making impossible things possible. The crew at BCC Press. Thank you, Andrew Heiss for your beautiful layout and typesetting, a truly important work. Clark, thank you for your beautiful design work. Carl, my husband, who read and re-read the manuscript, while also living beside me. John Evans, a dear reader, friend and writer who I admire. Kate Finlinson and Annie Blake who gave their precious time and encouragement. Joel Edwards for letting us live in his house with three wild children, and never saying an impatient word. Deborah Leopo who was there for all of it. Thank you, Rachel Hunt Steenblik, it was so special to work on our projects together. Thank you, Reija Rawle, a truest friend were there ever one, I'm grateful to have your words at the beginning of this book. Thank you, Diana Palmer for photographing me when I was most vulnerable. Thank you to my siblings and parents who are so supportive. Thank you to people, many of you strangers, who have gone out of your way to support me when it might have been easier to be silent. Thank you to my sister-in-law, Bree, who was diagnosed with this disease before me and has helped to guide the way. Thank you to the medical workers, and insurance workers, and so many people just doing their job that made the events of this book the easiest and the most gentle they could be.

Photo credit: Paige Smith

Ashley Mae Hoiland is the author and illustrator of the award-winning book, *One Hundred Birds Taught Me to Fly*. Her writing has appeared in many publications, both online and in print. She is the illustrator of *Mother's Milk* and *I Gave Her a Name*, both books of poetry by Rachel Hunt Steenblik. She received a BFA in painting and an MFA in creative writing from Brigham Young University. She is the co-founder of Mine To Tell, a space that teaches women to find their own strength through creative writing. More can be found on her website, Ashmae. com and at Minetotell.com. She currently lives in Santa Cruz, California with her husband and three children.

CPSIA information can be obtained
at www.ICGtesting.com
Printed in the USA
FSHW011250301019
63565FS